SINGLE AND WHOLE

SINGLE AND WHOLE

Temitayo Olaleye

WORD2PRINT

A Division of One-Touch Pro Ltd.

SINGLE AND WHOLE
Copyright © 2018 Temitayo Olaleye

All rights reserved. No part of this publication may be reproduced or transmitted in any form or by any means (electronic or mechanical) including photocopying, recording or any information storage or retrieval system without prior permission in writing from the publisher.

Scriptures are taken from the Holy Bible, King James Version KJV (Public Domain) or as otherwise noted.

First published in the United Kingdom in 2018 by
Word2Print
www.word2print.com
ISBN: 978-1-908588-34-0

A CIP catalogue record for this title is available from the British Library

Edit: Karis Kolawole, Karis Coaching & Consultancy

Cover Design: Supreme Core Media

Book Design: Supreme Core Media
www.supremecoremedia.com

Printed and bound by CPI Group (UK) Ltd, Croydon, CR0 4Y

CONTENTS

Dedication

Foreward

Acknowledgement

Introduction xi

CHAPTER 1: Being Single..1

CHAPTER 2: Finding Yourself......................................5

CHAPTER 3: Single and Whole in the Spirit..........19

CHAPTER 4: Single and Whole in the Soul............27

CHAPTER 5: Single and Whole in the Body 33

CHAPTER 6: Before You Are Found........................39

CHAPTER 7: The Formula: 1 + 1 = 1........................51

CHAPTER 8: A Final Word..65

The Single's Creed..69

FOREWORD

I count it a great privilege to present this book, 'Single and Whole' to you. The single phase of life is one that many misunderstand and, to some extent, despise. In many regards people see it as a necessary evil. They even come to the point of seeing themselves as someone waiting for marriage in order to be complete. Unfortunately, this wrong mindset has also infiltrated the circle of Christian believers and has become a fountain of compromise and misdirection. This is why I believe that this book is both timely and profound.

'Single and Whole' will bless you whether you are single, minister to singles, have singles in your life for whom you are concerned, or seek to encounter God's counsel on the reality of wholeness in the single life. The truths in this book do not disregard the sacred trust of marriage, but prepare whole singles for a wholesome marriage experience. I advise that you read prayerfully, seeking God's counsel to you from the pages of this book.

Be blessed!

David Oyedepo Jnr.

DEDICATION

To God, the Author and Finisher of my faith; the one who indites my heart with a good matter and inspires my hands to write.

To every man and woman, single and searching or not searching, or anyone who just needs answers, I have put this book together for you. I pray it blesses you the way I have been blessed writing it.

To the generation yet unborn, I pray this becomes a legacy to you and guides you along a lighted path.

ACKNOWLEDGEMENT

Throughout my life, I have been blessed from different sources, and I am humbled that God has given this powerful medium to give back out of the much I have received. But, I could not have done it alone without the many blessing channels that I am privileged to be connected to.

My biological parents – I am grateful for your love and support always and for putting me on the right path to life. Thank you, Dad and Mum.

Pastor David and Mrs Kemi Oyedepo – thank you for the great teachings, mentoring and the exemplary lives you lead. For your contribution to this book, I am eternally grateful.

Pastors Ayo and Elizabeth Adegbiji – thank you for your counsel, prayers and support at every stage. Thank you for always giving of yourselves and for all that you gave to bring this book alive.

My beloved brother in-love and my siblings: Joshua, Temilola, Temidayo and Temitope – thank you for allowing me to be myself and for all the lessons you help me learn.

My best friend Olaoluwa, thank you for always pushing me and encouraging me to keep going even when I didn't think I still had it in me. You always know the right thing to say!

Finally, my able editor, Mrs Karis Kolawole and the publishing team – I can't thank you enough for the excellent work on this project. Having you on board helped to spark the finishing. Thank God you said yes!

INTRODUCTION

We are all going through a process called life. One particular stage in this whole process that every human being, male or female, will pass through is SINGLENESS. If you are reading this book, you are either in this stage now or have moved on to marriage. You may be looking for knowledge for yourself or for the benefit of hindsight or to pass it to those who are still single. This book is essentially there to help anyone in their single season and anyone who carries a burden in their heart to counsel them.

Being single can be one of the most enriching times of anyone's life. It is a time to discover who we are in the present and to grow into who we are meant to be in the future. It is not a passive stage of life; we need to be proactive about making the most of it.

As with every other stage of life, it can be marked with challenges showing up in one form or another. So, it is important that we build our resilience and grow in wisdom so that we can handle those challenges. Our perspective of each stage of life is often influenced by how these challenges affect us. Some might describe their single stage using one or more of these words: loneliness, despair, anxiety, frustration, stigma (in some cultures), pressure, desperation, emotional imbalance and 'ticking biological clock'. Then, there are others who describe it with colourful language that communicates joy, excitement, hope and a great sense of satisfaction. I've experienced both sides of the coin.

It important to savour the beauty of being single and appreciate who we are and to develop every aspect of who we are meant to be. In this book, I share my journey of singleness. My journey was one that enabled me to experience wholeness even as a single person. Being whole boosts our value as we are as an individual on our own and as a partner in a marriage.

Single people can be quite vulnerable especially when they have attained what is deemed to be the 'the age' for marriage, and they are not yet in a relationship. Take for example, a young lady in her mid-twenties, who has completed a first degree and probably has a good job. To society, by default, she is 'old enough' for a relationship at the least. Pressure from others and herself to get into a relationship might push her in the wrong direction towards the wrong things. But, why 'hook up and mess up'?

I have found that what makes the difference is being single and whole in your spirit, soul and body. It changed my perspective and stirred up my determination to settle for nothing less than the very best for my life.

Bring in the Creator

You can't talk about being single and whole without bringing in the Creator of life, God! There is no point shying away from truths about God on this matter because He designed life. He gave the world the very first picture of singleness when He created man in the very first chapter of the Bible, and that is what inspired the title of this book. Therefore, you will find that I have used the Bible as my reference throughout this book, putting God at the centre of all the advice, insights and cautions I have shared.

If you are not used to the Bible, you do not need put this book down now. I believe you will still find the principles helpful for navigating through singleness and to a rewarding marriage (if that's what you want). Using my own experience, I show you how I have been able to put biblical principles into practice and ways you can avoid the pitfalls that can ruin your present and future. I show you how you can find yourself and become whole in your spirit, soul and body.

If being fruitful and whole is your goal in life, then come with me on this journey with an open mind and a heart ready to receive.

Chapter 1

BEING SINGLE

When God began the work of creation, as recounted in Genesis, the only living creature that was made in a singular form was MAN!

> *Then God said, 'Let Us make man in Our image, according to Our likeness; let them have dominion over the fish of the sea, over the birds of the air, and over the cattle, over all the earth and over every creeping thing that creeps on the earth.'* (Genesis 1:26)

God the Creator, first made various creatures in multiples – sea creatures, birds, land animals like cattle and creeping things, according to their kind (Genesis 1:20-25) until it was time to replicate His image in man. His image is male AND female embodied in one, a reflection of the plurality and wholeness of the Godhead. God created mankind in a state of wholeness. When He created woman, He didn't create from anywhere else; He took from man. So, I concluded that:

> *Singleness is a state of wholeness; mental, physical, emotional and psychological wholeness. It is a stage in the process of life.*

There is wholeness in singleness

This is hitting the nail on the head! Every idea in this book flows from this definition. It is interesting to realise that singleness is tied to wholeness. God, the Creator, is a purposeful being who doesn't engage in trial and error. The fact that man first appeared as a single being loaded with the potential of being 'double' and productive in every way, suggests that singleness is a stage in life that is characterised by wholeness.

I have realised, nonetheless, that it takes a lot of self-discipline to concentrate on creating a better and stronger you when it seems you are alone without a marital partner. The fact cannot be refuted that everyone needs somebody close and intimate. The Bible alludes to this. Ecclesiastes 4:9-10, NKJV

> *Two are better than one, because they have a good reward for their labour. For if they fall, one will lift up his companion. But woe to him who is alone when he falls, for he has no one to help him up.*

We cannot debunk or dispute this awesome statement pointing to marriage and its rewards.

My aim here is to explore how a person can handle the preceding stage before plunging into marriage. It is about keeping one's mental, physical, emotional and psychological parts together in wholeness in preparation for a great marriage once the singleness phase ends.

The next chapter will put the spotlight on the single person – you, I presume – before delving into the different aspects highlighted in my definition of wholeness. From here, this book becomes a lot more revealing.

Chapter 2

FINDING YOURSELF

Imagine the horror on a mother's face and the trauma in her heart when her grown-up daughter insists that she is not interested in any man, or a relationship? Well, I think my mother may be able to tell you about that! She was very concerned about me and always wanted to know why I was not seeing anyone or bringing anyone home at my age. Every time she asked, my response was always the same: 'I am not ready for that'. At some point, I started to understand her worry. So, I had to assure her that the fact that I was not seeing anyone at that moment, did not mean that I won't get married when the time is right and I'm ready. "I just don't need a boyfriend now", I'd say. After several conversations, I think she finally understood my point and allowed me to make my own decision; but, that didn't stop her from bringing up the issue again as would any concerned mother.

What is bad in being single?

I guess every concerned parent with children of 'marriageable age' out there would have a similar story. The one thing I believe parents in my mother's situation need to remember and understand is that we are all very different individuals, each with a unique assignment in life. Children of the same parents, even very identical twins, won't always have the same life journey. They are born to be different individuals who are on separate assignments. This reminds me of one of the reality shows that I have enjoyed on TV lately about the famous *Sister Sister* twins (Tia and Tamera). The show basically captures the twins' different lives as one is getting married, while the other is getting ready to bring a new life into the world. I am pretty sure these twin sisters have practically lived their whole lives together, doing the same thing at the same time, including acting, until the reality of life dawned on them and they had to embrace their differences. This is a big lesson parents need to learn. It would help them avoid a lot of needless heartache that they may experience in the process of expecting their children to be like someone else's, especially when it comes to choosing a life partner and marriage. The best you really can do is PRAY for them – pray that they make the right choice at the right time, so that they have no regrets in the future.

Also, pray for yourself as a parent. Pray that God should help you to be patient so that you do not push your children into making wrong or knee-jerk decisions just to avert the pressure you are mounting on them. Waiting on God the Creator for the best does take some time, a lot of grace and patience. I implore us all to wait: it pays in the end!

Playing the waiting game, the right way

Having looked at things from the parent's perspective, what then is the waiting adult to do in this period of waiting and in the face of the mounting pressure? Well, I guess the answer lies in the question: you wait! I have found some interesting dictionary meanings of the word WAIT. The following definitions, culled from the Encarta Dictionary, are helpful in explaining the waiting I'm talking about.

• **Do nothing:** *to stay in one place or do nothing for a period of time until something happens or in the expectation or hope that something will happen.* In contrast, the waiting I am talking about actually involves you DOING SOMETHING while you continue to expect what is to come. I explain this in more detail later.

• *To* **stop or slow down** *in order for somebody else to catch up.* I find this one particularly interesting.

Your period of waiting, whether as a man or a woman, could mean that you need to slow down for your other half to catch up with you, or vice versa! In other words, you could be the party that needs to do the catching up and, especially since we are first spiritual beings, it could mean a spiritual catch-up. It could also be mental, emotional, financial or even physical.

• *To be* **hoping** *for something or on the lookout for something.* Your waiting could also mean the obvious: you are on the lookout for the one that is to come. I believe this particular factor is key and is common to everyone in this waiting stage; you have an expectation and you are certainly keeping an eye out for it.

• *Be* **delayed or ignored** *for now: to be postponed or put off until later.* Do you feel left on the shelf? Waiting could also mean that you are being 'put on the shelf' by God. One of the things I have learnt in my walk with God is that when God is testing you, He seems to 'ignore' you! He puts you on the shelf and leaves you seemingly unnoticed for a while, just to see how you respond. In this instance, if God is delaying or ignoring a young lady, for example, she may begin to wonder why men don't seem to be looking her way. Sometimes, she may think she is not beautiful enough or she doesn't have what they are looking for, when she actually does, in the right proportions too! God could be testing you to watch your response! Check it!

• *To be* **ready** *or* **available** *for someone to take or use.* It is important to remember that in your period of waiting, you are either being prepared and made ready for someone to take or you are ready to be taken. What you are then waiting for is the 'someone' who is going to take you and you want to make sure it is not just someone, but the right someone.

The process of being made ready is very crucial and it is a process you have to pass through for the royalty in you to show forth, especially when you are heading for the palace! Sounds familiar? Remember Queen Esther and the rest of the maidens (Esther 2:12-13).

> *Each young woman's turn came to go in to King Ahasuerus after she had completed twelve months' preparation, according to the regulations for the women, for thus were the days of their preparation apportioned: six months with oil of myrrh, and six months with perfumes and preparations for beautifying women.*
>
> *Thus prepared, each young woman went*

to the king...

The maidens had to undergo a period of preparation that lasted for twelve months. I am sure the calendar for those twelve months was packed with activities. At the end of it all, they had to be certified as befitting for a king as powerful as King Ahasuerus. I believe the same thing should be expected of modern day kings and queens who have been appointed and ordained from above, children of the Most High, the King of kings. In order to embrace our position as royalty, we need to be prepared in this period of waiting. When we read that episode in detail, we see that Esther was the one who stood out among all the maidens. Could this be because she had enjoyed some favour with Hegai, the custodian in charge of the maidens, who had given extra measures to specially prepare Esther? Could it be that she knew the right preparation for what lay ahead? Does this say something? Perhaps, the more you put into the process of being prepared, the better your outcome?

• *To* **delay** *something because somebody is expected to arrive soon.* Lastly, our period of waiting could be a delay because somebody is expected to arrive soon. There is no better illustration for this than the **Parable of the Ten Virgins** that Jesus taught in Matthew 25:1-13.

Here again, we see another process of preparation. The virgins were made to wait for the bridegroom. Although, they had set out to meet the bridegroom, the Bible says that he was delayed, so they had to wait. Their own preparation took place when they set out to meet him: they did not know what to expect; as a matter of fact, they probably did not know that he would be late because they were going to MEET him. But, something happened and he was delayed. It was during this delay that their preparation or lack of it showed. And when he finally arrived, the ones who had prepared were ready to meet him. Unfortunately, those who were not were left behind because they still had some preparation to do, but it was too late! The time to prepare had passed and now it was time to be married!

From all the definitions that we have analysed and the scriptures we have looked at, we can see that the period of waiting is as important as the process of preparation involved. In fact, I think it is safe to say that the amount of preparation you put into your period of waiting determines whether the wait is worth it or not. It's almost like saying, 'The measure you give is the measure you get' or 'Your input determines your output'. The bottom line is that it is not enough to wait; you also need to put some preparation into the waiting because that is what makes it either a fruitful wait or an unfruitful one. This corresponds with what the Bible says about waiting, describing it with action words:

> *But those who wait on the Lord shall renew their strength; they shall mount up with wings like eagles, they shall run and not be weary, they shall walk and not faint.* Isaiah 40:31

> *The Lord is good to those who wait for Him, to the soul who seeks Him.* Lamentations 3:25

Self-discovery

One of the key elements of singleness is self, meaning your personality and individuality. It is impossible to enjoy singleness without self-discovery. You must recognise who you are as a person - your unique characteristics, gifts, abilities and everything that adds up to make you who you are. A combined knowledge of all these enables you to enjoy your singleness because you will embrace your uniqueness and what makes you different from the girl or lad next door. You have to love yourself, your body features, your life, your PURPOSE and your ASSIGNMENT in life before you are able to love or attach yourself to another. This is a priority.

Love your neighbour as you love yourself.
Matthew 22:39 (GWT)

According to the scripture above, in order to love your neighbour, you will first love yourself and in the same measure that you love yourself, you will be able to love your neighbour.

Love and Purpose

It's two days to Christmas and while in the mood of celebration, I remembered the story of a certain young lady whose life was completely changed when she agreed to change the course of man's destiny. Her name was Mary and we are introduced to her in Luke 1:26-27.

According to this story, Mary was a young lady who was in love and was engaged to be married to the love of her life. Well, that was until she received a visitor. An angel. God had chosen her to give birth to the Saviour of the whole world! What an honour bestowed on her, we might think. But, I bet she did not quite feel that way when she heard the rest of the assignment! She would become pregnant even though she was a virgin! How would she explain that? She had never known a man, yet she would soon be seen with a growing bump! Nobody was going to believe that, not even her fiancée. 'She must have been cheating on him' would be the general conclusion of most people, and how could she possibly prove them wrong? If Mary belonged to our generation, the news will quickly spread like wildfire on social media sites and I am sure it will get millions of likes, comments and reposts as it goes wildly viral! What an embarrassment for an innocent young lady!

But, Mary took on the assignment – despite the shame that came with it. She surrendered to the will of God and obeyed His instruction to the letter. However, she could not do it alone. Somebody had to be by her side and that person was the one who needed convincing, and God did just that (Matthew 1: 18-25). Joseph, her husband-to-be, also received a visitation and was instructed on what to do, and he also obeyed. He had a part in the assignment to birth the Saviour of the world and nurture him within a family unit, and he ran with it. It would not have been that easy for either of them, especially for Joseph, who had to become a father to a child he did not father.

Live in God's will as a single person

So, what's the lesson here? The will of God is not always your cup of tea! It's not usually what you dream of, or what you expect. In fact, in most cases, you already have your life planned out, or at least you have an idea of what direction you want your life to go, and when you receive God's instruction, it is hardly ever the same. When this happens, you must rejoice and humbly accept what God has for you, like Mary did (Luke 1:46-55). The will of God will take you beyond what you ever dreamed for your life. In Mary's case, all she had to do was surrender her life to the will of God and after nine months, she brought forth Heaven on earth. In other words, she carried Heaven in her womb. Mary was described as blessed because of this encounter (verses 28, 42 and 45). This tells me that the will of God for your life is what makes you blessed.

Also, God's will changes your name, title, status, etc. Mary, who would have been called 'shamed' or 'a disgrace', became highly honoured. She became married in the process and enjoyed greater honour even after the baby was born (Matthew 2:11, Luke 2:16-19). Not only was she given the privilege to conceive, incubate, nurture and give birth to the King, she was also a part of Jesus' earthly ministry. She had the privilege of motherhood over Jesus, to speak into His life and release Him into His destiny and by doing so, Jesus performed His first miracle (John 2:1-5) and went on to do exploits just as it had been foretold about Him. What a blessing!

As a young lady, Mary's story resonates with me

because I am at the point in my life when I am completely sold out to God's will and His plan for my life. I have tasted a little of what it means to be in the centre of His will and I have seen that there are many blessings attached to it. For this reason, I am prepared to go the long haul, doing His bidding, following His plans and obeying His instructions all the way and that includes the marital aspect of life. As a single person, it is very easy to come up with the perfect image of the one you want to spend the rest of your life with. However, you must be careful in making that decision because you need to know God's will for you. I know how daunting it is to have to wait first to hear God's will and then having to wait to see the manifestation. It does take time, but I tell you, it will be worth it in the end.

Going back to the story of the beloved Mary and Joseph, I am sure that Mary must have gotten to the point of being frustrated, wondering if Joseph will ever accept her with a baby that does not belong to him. Joseph, on the other hand, might have also been wondering where he got it wrong and what he did to deserve such a woman who was cheating on him. But, God stepped in and the story was different. They became a couple united by purpose, obedient to His will, and they enjoyed the blessing of being the parents to the Son of God, the Saviour of the whole world.

Fulfilment is in God's purpose and will

I don't know what God has mapped out for you as your life's journey but I can tell you that it is a glorious one (Jeremiah 29:11). Therefore, you must be ready to surrender to Him every step of the way, including making that ultimate decision of a life partner. This is because who you marry determines whether or not you fulfil your assignment in life. I say this because marriage generally takes a significant number of our years on earth, and it is in marriage that you find utmost fulfilment. So, if you are married to the wrong person, you will be so occupied trying to make that marriage work that you neglect what you should really be pursuing – fulfilment. If on the other hand, you are blessed to be married to someone with whom you share the same goal or vision, your sleeping and waking moments are spent in the hope of realising your God-given assignment just like Mary.

I am privileged to be surrounded by men and women who have been married for many years, and I see a lot of examples of couples who are enjoying the fulfilment of their assignment together, and that really inspires me. That has become my desire and I aspire to get there and I know that it takes listening for God's instructions and waiting on Him to make that happen. I have learnt that no matter how rocky the road may get (and it does get rocky), when a couple is united by purpose, it is difficult for the enemy to tear them apart even though he tries to. You become so focused on fulfilling the assignment that certain issues don't count. You are so purpose-driven that the opinions of others do not matter to you. All that matters is pleasing the Master and fulfilling the assignment so that you get a 'well-done' when all is said and done.

In summary, find yourself and discover your purpose. Your purpose will lead you to your partner, and your partner will lead you to your fulfilment in life. All it takes is waiting on God, listening for His instructions and committing yourself to obeying Him. May God help us to make the right choices in life in Jesus' name.

The Purpose Pun

When I was created, GOD had a PLAN for a JOURNEY with a PURPOSE which involves some PEOPLE and a SOMEBODY to travel with. I am to FOLLOW the PLAN for the JOURNEY and DISCOVER the PURPOSE and the PEOPLE and MEET the SOMEBODY to ARRIVE at the destination called FULFILLMENT!

Chapter 3

SINGLE AND WHOLE IN THE SPIRIT

I think back to when I first heard the call of God. I remember listening to so many preachers say that God will always use people with a 'past' or 'history' and turn their mess into a message. I remember thinking to myself and asking myself what mess God wanted to turn into a message in my life. I didn't have a 'past'; I was just an 18-year-old who was even yet to learn to face the harsh realities of life. Up until that time, I had been shielded under my parents' roof and the only places I knew to go to were school and church. No more! So how could God possibly use me? What would I be talking about if He did?

Little did I know that it was only just the beginning! A little while down the line, I went from one who had no 'past' into a big mess that I didn't realise I was in. Ignorance is no excuse yet I was ignorant. And, that event marked the beginning of the rest of my life.

Forgiveness and restoration

You never know what it means to be forgiven and restored until you have been taken through the process. I say process because that is what it is and the end result is change. Forgiveness and restoration, as I have experienced, is not a one-day event. It involves a series of actions in gradual stages to reach the end result. The first stage for me was **acceptance**. I had to step out of denial and step into acceptance, and admit I had been down a murky road. This for me was very difficult. How do I explain it? Once I was the innocent little girl who had no blemish to her name. Where did that girl go? It did not make sense. I was so sure I was in the right. I was sure God had been in it with me. So, coming to terms with the truth was a difficult step for me but I got there. It was as though a mirror was placed in front of me and all I could see was the fragments of my life sinking deeply into the pit. I was horrified. Was this really me? How did I get there? I had unanswered questions that only my Maker could answer and this meant finding my way back to Him. The journey back was a lot easier since I had accepted my wrong. He was right there with His loving arms waiting to receive me. I was broken and only His warm 'welcome back' embrace could fix me. In the words of the Psalmist, 'I cried out to the LORD with my voice and He heard me out of His holy hills' (Psalm 3:4). The Lord heard me and took me back like the prodigal child that I was.

Experiencing total forgiveness meant working hand in hand with God, to see myself through His eyes and be ready to **forgive myself** as He forgave me. I would not be human if it was easy for me to do this – see myself through God's eyes when I had just made a mess of my life and the grace He gave to me! But, the Lord is ever faithful and merciful. He held me in His arms and everyday was a new day. Not that I did not regress every now and then, but my Heavenly Father was patient with me. He did not toss me out or leave me to myself. I could feel His reassuring presence every step of the way. I came to terms with all that had happened and I realised that if God could forgive me. Who am I then not to forgive myself? After all, I had sinned against Him; it was His commandments I had disobeyed and His grace I had taken for granted. Forgiving myself also meant being able to enjoy His love all over again and be God's little girl again.

The next stage on my restoration journey was to **forgive others**. I was so hurt and offended that this became the hardest part of it all. I remember the days I had taken time out to wait on God and get used to hearing His voice again. When it was time to talk to God and pray for my healing and the forgiveness of those who had hurt me, I found it very difficult. I would just lament, uttering negative words as I prayed. I would completely break down in tears in the place of prayer because although I was in the process of being healed, all I wanted was for them to have a taste of their own medicine. At the same time, I also knew that God is merciful and He alone knows how to deal with every one of us. That made it all the more painful but I had to let go. This again was a gradual process and my Father was always patient and loving through it.

I knew I had reached a good place in my healing process when I was ready to **talk to someone**. I remember walking down the road one lovely afternoon when the thought of all the pain I had been through flashed through my mind, and all I could do was smile. I did not burst into another round of tears, neither did I have an emotional breakdown. I knew right there and then that I was ready to speak to someone. Note that all through the initial stages of the process, I ran to God alone and because He had carried me through it, I was ready and able to share with man in the latter stages. The mistake we make most times when we have strayed is that we run to man first to 'confess' our sins. But, what can a fellow human being do? Man has no power to forgive us. That man or woman you are confessing your sins to before going to God did not create you, neither did he or she give you the laws and commandments that you disobeyed. God did. Hence, He should be your first point of contact when you have disobeyed His commandments. He alone knows how best to chastise you and empower you to live above sin. The best that any human being can do for you in that situation is to judge you and when they chastise you, it is nothing like the chastisement that the Lord will give to you. Above all, man has no power to forgive and restore you like Christ would do. Christ died and shed His blood for the remission of your sins. He paid the price; man did not. If peradventure you are reading this book and you are wondering, 'How do I talk to God?' or 'I don't know if God hears me', I suggest that you speak to someone who can guide you in this. Find a Bible-believing church around you and speak to a spiritual leader who can pray with you if you feel comfortable to do so.

I could speak to my mentor and spiritual leader because at that crucial time, I needed a covering as God was carrying out the work of restoration. Somebody needed to be aware and be my pillar in the place of prayer and help me focus on making the right decisions. I thank God for the life of my mentor – a mother indeed. She listened like she knew what I was coming to say even though she was shocked and devastated just as I had expected her to be. She was loving, compassionate and forgiving through it all and reassured me that God has forgiven me and that was all that mattered. She prayed for me like a mother would for her prodigal child and shared communion with me. This was a physical manifestation of what had already taken place in the spirit realm. My Heavenly Father had welcomed and received me back home and laid His hands on me which also translated into what happened in this meeting with my spiritual covering. The Spirit of God is one and the same.

Get out of the mess

The 'mess' I am describing here is sin. I do not know how deep you have gone into acts of sin and how unforgivable you may think it is. I have good news for you. You have a loving Father who is ever ready to forgive and restore you back in His arms. I can tell you this because I have been there. He forgave me, lifted me out of the miry clay and set my feet on a rock. Guess what? He can do the same for you if you return to Him. This step is very essential in your journey to wholeness. Your spirit-man must be standing free from sin and every weight before anything else can happen. I implore you to stop for a moment right now, confess those sins and rededicate your life to God, the Master Builder of your destiny, before you continue this journey. Say these words out loud:

> *Lord Jesus, I come to You today. I know that I have sinned against You by violating Your commandments and allowing myself to be defiled by sin. Have mercy on me, dear Lord and draw me back to Yourself. I repent of every unrighteous act I have taken part in... (name them – be honest and specific).*
>
> *Please forgive me. I want to experience Your forgiveness and be made whole again by Your Spirit. Help me Lord to walk blamelessly and uprightly before You, in Jesus name. Amen.*

If you said those words with all sincerity of heart, know that God has heard you and you are now forgiven. Now take those steps I mentioned previously to complete your restoration process. You must forgive yourself, forgive the ones who hurt you and then talk to a trusted spiritual leader or mentor about your experience. I can guarantee that you will never remain the same. You will feel like a brand new person and it will appear as though that chapter of your life never existed.

SINGLE AND WHOLE

Wholeness in the spirit is important to singleness because man is primarily a spirit with a soul that lives in a body. In other words, your spirit is who you really are. Your body is simply the house that carries your spirit. Therefore, if you are to be truly single and whole, your spirit must first be made whole. Your spirit must be connected to the One who gives it life, hence the need for salvation as a first step. Now that you have completed that first step, I say congratulations! You are well on your way to total wholeness.

Chapter 4

SINGLE AND WHOLE IN THE SOUL

The soul is an integral part of your being. I have heard someone say that the soul is the seat of the emotions, intellect and will. Therefore, I don't think we can deal with being whole in the soul without dealing with emotions, and vice versa. By soul, I am referring to that part of you that receives and responds to produce an emotion or a feeling.

Emotional well-being

Your emotional health is very important if you are to enjoy and experience wholeness in your mind and soul. A lot of times, we pay much more attention to our bodies than we do to our minds because we somehow believe that being healthy only has to do with our physical body. Good health incorporates all parts of our being including our mind and soul.

3 John 1:2 (NKJV)

> *Beloved, I pray that you may prosper in all things and be in health, just as your soul prospers.*

If this scripture is anything to go by, we can see that our ability to prosper in all things depends on our soul prospering. Another translation puts it this way:

3 John 1:2 (NIV)

> *Dear friend, I pray that you may enjoy good health and that all may go well with you, even as your soul is getting along well.*

In other words, your soul needs to be getting along well as much as the other parts of your being, if not more. If things are not well with the soul, the body barely has any strength to feed on, and that is why your soul has to feed off your spirit which is, of course, the strongest part of your being. Everyone has a soul, but what makes each soul different is what it feeds on from the spirit. This then transcends to the body to give us a full human life.

So, why talk about emotional health and well-being? As I have already explained, our emotions are based in the soul which means they are regulated by what we feed the soul. If your spirit is well-fed by the Word of God on a daily basis, it passes its nourishment on to the soul and the end result is positive. We find ourselves full of joy and happiness (emotion). Does this mean we don't get upset sometimes? Of course, not! It just means that when situations turn around for the not-so-good, we are able to control our emotions even when we have every reason to be sad or upset. Such is the power of the soul.

Letting go and saying no

Maintaining your emotional health sometimes means reducing the weight that you carry within your emotions. It may mean taking off the excess load on your mind – work-related issues, personal issues, hurts and aches from the past, or even some friendships. You can sometimes find that one or a combination of any of these places a burden or a heavy weight on you that you need not carry. I personally had to deal with a number of them. Two key principles come to play here: saying no and letting go

I call them principles because that is what they become once you have put them into practice over and over again. Although they may seem so simple, they are by far the hardest things to do in life. They are hard for several reasons especially because they mostly involve the things or people that mean the most to you, or that you find solace in.

Saying "no"

How do you say no to the people you have never had a reason to say no to, the same people who 'need' you or the support you give to them all the time? Saying no doesn't always mean saying no when a friend or loved one asks you to do something. It could mean saying no to the things that you do that they don't even have to ask you to do. In the case of the latter, you are saying no to yourself, and in essence, to them and to those things that you do so easily even without being asked. You do them out of a kind, loving heart but nobody sees or appreciates them.

I remember a period in my life when I was seemingly obsessed with certain friendships. I was always the one to call these friends to 'check up' on them and ask about their plans, etc. I would then get so annoyed and frustrated when they don't reciprocate the gesture. I had to settle down and ask myself why I felt that way each time. Sometimes I would even cry because I felt like no one cared about me. As time went by, my eyes began to open. I discovered that I was simply battling with insecurity and a low self-esteem, so much that I felt like I needed the company of these friends to keep myself happy. When I realised this truth, I began to say "no" to myself regarding the desire to seek comfort in friendships that I did not necessarily need. Saying no to myself allowed me to say no to those sour friendships.

Letting go

Letting go is a whole new level but you will also find that they are both related. When you say no, it may also become necessary to let go and turn a blind eye to what you have said no to. This requires a lot of self-discipline and can be very painful, but you do it because you have to in order to stay healthy emotionally.

From my experience, it is never the easiest thing to do. Many times, I questioned myself because I thought I was just being mean and heartless. But, I had to constantly remind myself that the love that I have for those people and those things has not diminished. I just have to do this in order to love myself first. For love to be effective, it must begin with loving one's self. I have to love myself well in order to be able to love others, and loving myself means that I have to look after myself and my well-being. I had to let go of a lot of friendships and, need I say, it was a hard thing to do but I am

SINGLE AND WHOLE

better for it.

You are not ready to move into complete wholeness until you say no to and let go of those unnecessary weights that you are carrying, either for yourself or for a loved one. You must do it, not just once but as many times as you need to in order to free your soul from the burden. You must know what they are, how to spot them and how to react quickly to them. This is because the longer they are around you, the more they will start to feel like a part of you. I cannot tell you what those things or even people are in your life. You are the master of your own life in this situation. Engage the help of the Holy Spirit to help you identify those weights in your life. I must warn you, however, that it could be the relationship or friendship that you hold most dearly, or it could even be something you don't realise exists in your mind. That's why you need the Holy Spirit to help you spot them and respond to them appropriately. When you have done this, you are ready for your wholeness.

Chapter 5

SINGLE AND WHOLE IN THE BODY

1 Corinthians 6:19 (NKJV) says:

> *Or do you not know that your body is the temple of the Holy Spirit who is in you, whom you have from God, and you are not your own?*

You might already know this scripture and refer to it every time you talk about your body, but I present it to you again and hopefully, with a new light. I am no expert on the anatomy of the human body, neither am I able to teach you how to look after your body because the fact is, it is yours to look after. All I want to emphasise here is that God has given you that body to be His house so that He can stay connected to you. It is extremely unique to you – your figure, contour, size etc. You are uniquely endowed so much that no one in the entire universe has the same fingerprints as you. How amazing! He made you so unique and different to the girl or lad next door, and very special to Him. God cares about your body so much that He even numbered the hair on your head (Luke 12:7) and He says He wants you to be in health (3 John 1:2). So, dear friend, what's your reason for not looking after your body and keeping it healthy the way God intends it to be?

Whole in the body

When I talk about wholeness in the body, I don't just mean a body that is free from sickness, even though I believe that God is more than able to heal any sickness and make you whole. I am also talking about loving and embracing every curve and blemish, and loving yourself enough to give your body what it needs to house the greatness of God inside you and nurturing it until it shows.

Some instances in the Bible where the sick were not only healed but were made whole by taking another step may perhaps help to paint a clear picture. Firstly, Mark 5:25-34 (KJV) tells the story of a certain woman who is introduced not by her name, but by her circumstance. She had been battered and broken by this affliction so much that it had become her identity. She heard about Jesus and she said, "If I may touch but His clothes, I shall be whole" (verse 28). Indeed, she touched Him and she felt her healing process begin but it did not end there. Jesus had to see her; she needed to step forward and surrender to Him for complete healing so that she could be whole. Jesus spoke a word that sealed the healing and indeed she was whole, ready to face her destiny.

Another story I'd like you to think about is that of the ten lepers who we meet in Luke 17:11-19. These men needed healing and they cried out to Jesus and He healed them. Out of the ten, only one of them was made whole because he did something the others did not do. He stepped out and surrendered to the awesome power that healed him and because of that, he was made whole.

Someone may ask, what is the difference between being healed and being whole from these examples? After all, they all received their healing. Being whole means you have received the same power that healed you to rise above that affliction or any other problem that may come your way. Being whole means you have experienced the love of God in your innermost part and that drives your devotion to Him to a whole new level. Wholeness means you are more committed to God than you ever were and you are willing to do anything to please Him, including looking after His temple and keeping it clean from all debris and decay.

How do you look after your body?

1. Feed it right. What goes inside your body on a daily basis? What are you feeding God's treasured temple every time you open your mouth to take a bite? What benefits do your organs and body systems derive from the food you eat and what you drink? I will not dwell too much on this as this is just food for thought. I will leave you to count the cost and the calories!

2. Exercise it right! Bodily exercise profits a little (1Timothy 4:8). A little you may say, but the point is that it profits. So, get moving!

3. Dress it right. Dressing appropriately cannot be overemphasised. I will put it this way: you are addressed by the way you are dressed. So, dress the way you want to be addressed. It's just that simple but it doesn't stop there. I encourage you to adorn yourself gorgeously and present yourself like the treasure that you are in your manner of dressing. However, don't get carried away by or be too focused on your outward appearance alone.

1 Peter 3:3-4 (NKJV)

> *Do not let your adornment be merely outward—arranging the hair, wearing gold, or putting on fine apparel—rather*

let it be the hidden person of the heart, with the incorruptible beauty of a gentle and quiet spirit, which is very precious in the sight of God.

God is interested in your all-round health and wholeness. So, yes, look fabulous and fly; it brings Him glory. Nevertheless, do not neglect the most important radiance that He expects from you: your inner beauty. The outward appearance can be deceptive but whatever is on the inside reveals much more about you. In actual fact, I would say that if you focus more on building the inner man, decorating and adorning the outward would be a breeze and you will find great delight in looking after your body.

Dress the part

A part of being whole is not just following the trend, but setting your own standards for your dressing, looks, diet, style, scent, etc. You must know what works for you and above all what is good for you. I remember growing up with this impression that my natural hair is too tough and I just couldn't wait to be older so I could relax it. It didn't help that I went to a school where permed hair was prohibited. I just wanted to be out of there so I could do whatever I wanted to my hair. On graduating from secondary school, what was the first thing I did? I turned my hair into a softer texture. Little did I know that was the beginning of the damage that was about to ruin my hair. A few years later, my hair was completely damaged and constantly falling out until I couldn't stand it any longer. I then decided it was time to go back to my natural tresses. This was even before it became a popular trend as we now see it. Many more women are buying into the #*mynaturalhairisbeautiful* trend which, of course, is a wonderful thing to see. My point is that whatever you choose to wear, wear it because it works for you and not just because others are wearing it that way.

Know your body and love it well enough to look after it. Carry your body like the temple of God that it is and present yourself like the royal diadem that you are. Consciously avoid any permanent or even temporary damage that may come to it through sin or anything worldly. Remember, your body is an essential vehicle for arriving at the wholeness we describe and much more, the fulfilment you desire.

Chapter 6

BEFORE YOU ARE FOUND

We have discussed what being whole looks like. How then do we carry on in that wholeness especially in making life-changing decisions such as choosing a partner? What should I look out for in myself or in a potential partner? Let us look at some pointers you may want to consider to help you make this all-important decision. I have taken this from a teaching by late Dr Myles Munroe. He outlined the qualities of the man and the woman at the forefront of creation. He called them the beginning man and the beginning woman, according to their assignments as told in Genesis 2.

The beginning man

1. The beginning man is a man with a clear self-image, knowledge of his purpose and an unwavering confidence in his Creator.

2. The beginning man is first in the presence of God, where the core and essence of his being is formed. He must be found in God's presence, not anywhere else.

3. He must be working. He must love working because God gave him work to do as soon as he was created.

4. He must be a cultivator. He must cultivate everything he comes in contact with including his woman! If she is not quite the way he wants her to be when he finds her, he must be prepared to cultivate her into his ideal. For example, if he thinks she is not polished enough, he must do all it takes to carry out the polishing even if it means enrolling her into a school and paying for her to be polished to his taste.

5. He must be a protector. He must protect everything in his care: his woman, home, family, children, everything committed to his hands must be protected.

6. He must know the Word of God and teach it to his woman. God gave the beginning man the instructions to guide his existence in the Garden of Eden (Genesis 2:16-17). It is the duty of the man to share that knowledge with his woman.

And then in verse 28, God said that it is not good for this man to be alone. In other words, a man who is not in the presence of God, is not working, is not a cultivator, and is not a protector; might as well be alone. What does he need a helper for? He is a time waster. He will be indecisive. He will string a woman along and make her think he cares about her but, really and truly, he has no long-term plans because he is yet to discover why he needs her. Ladies, beware of such a man!

Do you fit the beginning man?

On the other hand, if you are a man that matches all the attributes of the beginning man, then you should not be alone. You must be aware that God has taken a rib out of you to create your 'womb-man'. He has equipped her very well, formed her so beautifully and has placed in her all that is required to complete you. As He parades her before you, what are you saying? Are you still thinking perhaps little tweaking needs to be done? Are you questioning God's master creative power, or are you still asleep under the effects of the sedatives from the Master's surgery? Well, it is time to wake up and give the Master matchmaker an answer. What He has placed before you, like it or not, is your perfect match. It is now up to you to do the cultivating and the polishing to suit you. Yes, He has given you the power to do so; take it! Did you not hear the response of the beginning man? He said: "This is now the bone of my bone and the flesh of my flesh and she will be called woman because she was taken out of me" (Genesis 2:23). God did not tell him what she was called. He liked what he saw because he knew God would not have made any error, and he quickly gave Him a response before He could take her away. Adam only added a prefix to his name and named her after him (man became woman). In fact, I believe this is why women take on their husband's surname. So, what are you waiting for? Give her a name; your name! Finish the work. God has made it so easy for you but He won't do it for you!

Do you fit the beginning woman?

Now, let's take a look at some of the characteristics of the beginning woman. I must say, having studied this woman, I really admire her and I aspire to be like her.

1. She is a helper. She helps her man to fulfil his vision, and not destroy it. She does not tell him how to run his life because she knows her place as a helper, and a helper does not run the show. She makes it her duty to study her man and she is constantly asking questions, not irritating or criticising him. She is able to shape him into an 'ideal' man if he is not already one. Not only does she see his vision, she also understands it and submits her vision to his. As a woman, if you meet a man with a vision, submit your vision to his and leave it at that. This is how to be blessed.

2. She is a producer. She reproduces whatever her man gives to her. With groceries, she produces a meal. With sperm, she produces a child. With money, she produces resources and investments. With a house, she produces a home. With affection, she produces love. She is always producing.

3. She is an incubator. She receives, expands and gives it back. As a woman, you must be careful what you receive from external sources such as friends because what you receive, you will incubate and end up dumping on your man.

4. She is an encourager. She is constantly encouraging her man and giving him the push he needs to move forward, to try harder or try again.

5. She is a receiver. Whenever she sees a good thing, she desires it and she must receive it. Ladies, you must appreciate whatever you receive, no matter how little it may seem.

6. She is a prophetess. By nature, the beginning woman is a prophet. She always has a word because she has incubated what she has received and she multiplies it and has something to give back.

As I write this, the Proverbs 31 woman comes to mind. There are a number of similarities between the beginning woman described above and the Proverbs 31 woman. However, I must point out that the most common denominator, which is not necessarily spelt out but underlies the character of both women, is the fear of God.

The total woman

Some years ago, while I was at the university, there was a day when I was on my own in my room and the Holy Spirit began to speak to me about the TOTAL WOMAN! He said that there is a difference between being a virtuous wife and a total woman. A total woman is in a higher position than the virtuous wife because God does not need a virtuous wife; only a man does. What God requires is a total woman and it takes being a total woman to really become a virtuous wife. As a single lady, you should prepare yourself towards being a total woman. That way, when you become married, you are already loaded with virtues to display.

Who then is a total woman?

Proverbs 31:30 says,

> *Charm is deceitful and beauty is passing, but a woman who fears the LORD, she*

shall be praised.

The fear of God is what makes you a total woman and when God sees you as total woman, you will be a virtuous wife to ANY man i.e. a combination of the beginning woman and the Proverbs 31 wife. As I learnt that day and as I continue to learn, obedience is a proof of your fear of God. When you truly fear God, you obey all His instructions and He can trust you, as we see in Ecclesiastes 12:13:

> *Let us hear the conclusion of the whole matter: Fear God, and keep his commandments: for this is the whole duty of man.*

So, my dear woman, in order to make the mark of the beginning woman and ultimately, the total woman, you must fear God with every fibre of your being. Know His will and do it. Serve Him with your life, and love Him with your all. Not only will your man find you, but he will also find in you a virtuous woman.

Maturity

Maturity, both spiritual and emotional, is a great key to attaining and maintaining wholeness. Knowing God's plan and having a vision for your life is one thing, but having the wisdom and the maturity to handle whatever life throws at you is another. This is because things will happen in life that were not part of your plan but you must be ready to deal with them. Don't expect to go through life without a glitch because the bigger your vision, the stronger the opposition you will meet on your journey. Look at the story of Joseph in Genesis 49. He was carrying a clear, God-given vision but look at how many oppositions he had to tackle, including the temptation from Potiphar's wife and hatred from his own brothers. The good news is that you can be sure of victory at the end of the battle. However, you must be ready to fight!

Maturity has nothing to do with age. You might be older than Methuselah and have the mind of a teenager or you could be a young David and have the mind of a wise king. The Bible assures us that from salvation, we already have the mind of Christ. What we do with that mind, coupled with the experiences we gather and learn from in life, goes a long way in preparing us for its battles. You must challenge yourself. You must step out of your comfort zone. Many times, the reason why we refuse to come out of our comfort zone is fear – fear of failing or making a mistake. I have learnt from experience that it is alright to make mistakes. What we must not do is fail to learn from those mistakes or worse off, go ahead and repeat the same mistakes. I believe that God expects us to learn from our mistakes, otherwise, why would He prepare a second chance for us? Proverbs 24:16 says that, 'For a righteous man falls seven times, and rises again, but the wicked stumble in time of calamity.' If you fall, get up, shake off the dust and remember God already made provision for that.

When love hurts

Some of us have at one time or another had to deal with the sordid experience of heartbreak. The common saying, 'The only ones you give the power to hurt you are the ones you love', is virtually true. When you love, you make yourself vulnerable enough to be hurt; you are giving yourself up and letting down your guard which sometimes opens the door to such heartbreak.

If this has ever been your experience, you need to ensure that you are completely healed from those past experiences before you proceed to loving another. You don't want to carry the pain or the debris from your previous experience to another person because it will affect both of you negatively. I have found from personal experience that you become so guarded that even when your newly found love is doing their best to love you, you are unable to receive what they give. After some time, frustration kicks in on their part and they can no longer take it and they might walk away. Only a truly persistent and patient person can endure such a hostile circumstance of loving someone who is not reciprocating it. Don't wait until it's too late before you open up and make yourself vulnerable again for the one who wants to love you. Remember that just because you have been hurt a few times before does not necessarily mean everyone is out there to hurt you. You must learn to trust again and allow the Holy Spirit to love through you. That way, you will experience true love.

And, if you are privileged to love someone who has been hurt before, I implore you to be gentle, patient and kind. Be a true example of love as outlined in 1 Corinthians 13. It takes a process to heal any wound, some longer than others. It may not be the easiest journey of all but be determined to see them through it. Sometimes, people don't even realise how much they are still hurting until someone comes along to love them. Even then, they still don't know it because they are so guarded and will do anything to prevent anyone getting in to hurt them again. Hence, the need for your patience. Continue to reassure them of the sincerity of your love. Pray for them and support them as they become whole again without being too pushy about it, as they may be in denial. It takes grace to go through this process, the kind that is available through the Holy Spirit. Whatever you do, don't rush them and don't be in a hurry to leave them either. You could be the miracle they have been praying and waiting for to complete their healing process.

Chapter 7

THE FORMULA: 1 + 1 = 1

Now that you have found out how to be whole, let's talk about relationships! The formula to bear in mind here is 1 + 1= 1, which signifies two whole individuals, as described in the preceding chapters, coming together to make unified wholeness.

Relationships require a lot of work and you have to be ready to put in the work in order to make it work. In my study of biblical relationships, I learnt a number of lessons from the exemplary life of Ruth and how she managed her relationships:

1. In establishing and cultivating relationships, don't make commitments too hastily. Wait until you understand the major implications of any commitment you make to another person.

2. Practice loyalty and understand that this means putting others ahead of self, personal advantage and comfort.

3. Once you've made such commitment, do not back out without a good reason.

4. Be faithful and godly. Be determined and be persistent in your commitments.

5. Learn servanthood. God calls us to serve those we love. Believe that He will honour those who relate to others with a servant's heart.

6. Relate with great love, humility and respect.

God's leading versus your choice

One thing I have been coming across quite a lot lately is the subject of God's involvement in your choice of marriage partner. I have read quite a bit on this, and I understand that God limited His involvement in man's choice of a marriage partner after Adam tried to blame Him for choosing Eve for him. My understanding of Adam's situation is that God presented Eve to him after He created her as a 'help-meet' for him. It was entirely Adam's decision to name her after himself and, as we now know it, marry her. God had nothing to do with that part. Yet when things fell apart for the man, he had the nerve to blame God for his own decision to make the woman his. I am not saying that Adam was wrong to have married Eve. After all, God made her specifically to be a help-meet for him. He had the right to reject her, keep her at arm's length, or maybe make her a co-worker. But, he chose to take her in as his wife. I believe that based on that decision, it was up to him to groom her and teach her the same instructions that God had already given him, rather than blame God for his failings which were facilitated by her. What I am saying in essence is that we have a say in choosing who we marry and who we decide to join ourselves with on the journey to fulfilment of purpose. However, I also believe that being totally surrendered to the will of God gives us an advantage in making this all-important life decision. If we are asking for the will of God for other areas of our lives and God gives us that, He is also able to give us His will for our marital destiny, which is pivotal to our fulfilment in all other areas.

We must understand, however, that even though God empowers our decision-making when we are in His will and He points us in the right direction to go, it is entirely up to us how we manage the decision and what follows it. For example, if I choose a career because I believe that is where God has called me to be a blessing to humanity, I am required to go further and learn all I can or need to know about that field in order to excel and reach the people God has sent me to. If I fold my hands and do nothing because God has led me to or 'chosen' that career for me, that will only amount to failure because the fulfilment I seek will not meet me folding my hands. I must apply myself and give all diligence to becoming the best that I can be in my assignment.

The same thing goes for marriage. Just because God has led someone into our lives as a marital potential or partner does not automatically guarantee success in the marriage. We must put our heads together and decide how we want to excel in the journey together, and allow God to lead us every step of the way. We must find out all we can about the other person and do due diligence on them before we begin the journey. What can you or can you not handle about them? What is the absolute deal breaker for you? God will not tie you to a person who has characteristics that you already know you are not prepared to deal with. Hence, the choice is totally yours, not His.

If you decide to proceed into marriage with someone that God brought your way or led you to, it is expected that you have both mutually reached that decision and neither party is going into the marriage because "God said". Let's not attempt to drag the name of God in the mud. Make sure you have reached that decision yourselves and you both know where you are heading. The good news is that God has prepared the way

The Formula: 1 + 1 = 1

ahead and He is able to make every grace abound to you in your journey together when you call on Him and continue to rely on His help. However, enjoying the fullness of His grace also requires a willingness to work at it.

Marriage requires two whole individuals who are coming together to enjoy complete wholeness and fulfil destiny together. Therefore, it is very important that you become whole before you begin to look for a life partner. Your wholeness will enable you to make an informed decision and know exactly what your potential spouse should be – whole. Even if they are not there yet, you will know exactly what to do or how to help them reach that level because you are already whole. Together, you become a formidable force and can accomplish whatever God commits into your hands.

Someone to love?

You go to bed one day, and you wake up the next and you realise that you have someone to love and who loves you back. He or she is the most amazing person in the world, in your own eyes. Everything you dreamt of, prayed and waited for is finally in your life! You are excited! You are suddenly no longer single and you can join the 'league' of those who are in a relationship and you will finally have something to talk about when your friends are talking about their beau. What a thrill!

Many times, we get so caught up in the excitement of having someone to love that we actually don't get round to loving them before things get out of hand. When two people come together and agree to walk together in such a relationship that will lead to marriage, they come with various misconceptions, ideals and expectations. We all have in our minds what we want our relationship with our spouse to be like, and what we want them to be able to do for us. In some cases, we also have in our minds what we want to do for or with them e.g. go out on dates, hang out with friends, exchange gifts, talk, and some even go as far as sharing physical intimacy! All of these are based on the standards that have been set in the world we live in. We need to come out from these worldly expectations and follow the standard from the Bible, which is to actually show our spouse love in its genuine form. What do I mean by this? How can we really love someone without doing all these things that many people do in a relationship? I am not objecting to going out on dates and hanging out when you are in a relationship. No! I just want us to get to the consciousness of truly loving the one we claim to love and this is how:

1. Pray for the one you love. You will do well to continually lift him or her in prayers. Speak into his or her life on the altar of prayer the things you want to see them become.

2. Show your love. As much as spending time with your loved one helps to develop closeness in a relationship, don't get complacent because you feel you see him or her often enough. Think of creative ways to show you love them every time you see. And remember, this does not have to involve anything sexual as you make efforts to abstain from that. Christ demonstrated His love for us through His actions–He gave His life for mankind. Your actions towards them will be the demonstration of your love.

3. Say it. Although, I have mentioned that love is in actions, you must also bear in mind that your spouse-to-be needs to hear you say it. This is a great tip particularly for men. It has been said that while men are moved by what they see, women are moved by what they hear. Your woman needs to hear you say how much you love her, in as many or as few words that you can gather, as often as you can gather them. Continue to say it! Use kind words!

4. Be patient. We have established that we all have different notions when we come together in a relationship. Some of these have been formed from past experiences, or even knowledge gained. Your spouse may not always see things the same way you do, hence you must take time to work through situations that you don't immediately agree on. Just because he or she doesn't see it from your point of view now does not mean that will not change, or that both of you will continue to disagree. Allow some time for them to get a better understanding of the issue as you are both learning from and about each other.

5. Correct graciously. This follows the previous point. Neither of you is perfect. We all have our faults and intolerances. When your loved one has erred, don't be quick to retaliate or tell him or her off for doing a wrong. Deal with the situation as mentioned above. Allow time for the heat of the moment to cool down and then calmly approach the matter, without trying to bring up your partner's faults. Speak to him or her as you would expect to be spoken to in order to find a way forward in the situation. Aim for peace.

6. Respect him or her. Respect, as they say, is reciprocal. Show respect and you will earn respect. Respect to a man could mean submission as the Bible teaches. You respect or submit to anyone you love, just as you will love someone that you respect. Love and respect go hand in hand.

Maintain your spiritual edge

A relationship with the opposite sex, especially one with an end in mind, should be handled with utmost spirituality. In my view, just as marriage is spiritual, the relationship that leads to marriage is also spiritual. To make the most of this spiritual adventure, we must prepare for it and walk in the spirit (Galatians 5:16). The enemy knows when you are prepared, especially when you are determined to keep the bed undefiled in your journey. His aim is to destroy the glorious destiny that God has pre-packaged for you in marriage before you get there. So, he will do whatever it takes to get you to either fall or fail in the relationship. The Bible admonishes us to give no place to the devil because if he finds a loophole and enters your heart, he will only come in and take over. I used to think that the devil makes a grand appearance or announces his visit beforehand, but I have learnt otherwise. This cunning creature comes like a thief in the night, unnoticed and unannounced, especially when you are very focused on doing the will of God in all areas of your life including your relationship. He knows that his plans are overruled by God's plans any day. Anyone who is following God's plan automatically becomes his enemy because he wants to prevent the execution of the plan of God, which ultimately sees him defeated. This is why we must be watchful (1 Peter 5:8) and engage our weapons of warfare constantly to avoid any form of carnality in relationships (2 Corinthians 10:4).

You may think, 'It's just a kiss; we're not going any further than that' but remember that all the devil needs is a loophole and he is coming right in. He is waiting for the moment when you are off your guard to prowl in. We cannot afford to give him such luxury. We must be on the watch at all times. Sexual sins as described in the Bible do not necessarily take place on a bed. Jesus said they begin in the heart (Matthew 5:27-30). It is what you allow into your heart that begins the process of corrupting the seed of righteousness that is already inside you.

Apart from the danger of committing sexual sins, another consequence of trivialising your spiritual walk in a relationship is that it also opens the door for all sorts of evil including confusion, strife, anger and every manifestation of the flesh (James 3:16, Galatians 5:19). When such things are present, you begin to spend a lot of time and energy dealing with conflicts and issues when you should be focused on the purpose for which God brought you together. You begin to see different sides to your intended spouse that suddenly

The Formula: 1 + 1 = 1

don't go down too well with you, and you find several reasons why things are not working; the devil simply puts confusion in your midst.

How far is too far when you are in love?

Have you ever found yourself asking this question? I know I have! As believers in courtship, we already know God's expectation regarding physical intimacy. Sex is ONLY for the married. Every form of physical intimacy is encompassed within that and should be kept until marriage. You are then left in a situation where you have developed a bond both on a spiritual and a mental level and you are now physically attracted to your beloved, though still unmarried. How can you let them know this while keeping the bed undefiled as the Scriptures admonish? This is a question I have pondered on every now and then and it is not easy especially when you have both decided to wait it out. While studying on this, I discovered that you have gone too far when you have crossed the lines of sharing a goodnight kiss!

It is advisable to not dwell on the subject too much. When you dwell on it, you not only invite the temptation but you also begin to listen to the tempter's suggestions because he is also aware of your struggles as a believer. You and your future spouse must agree together on this and decide what 'too far' will be because of varying sexual responses. It could mean deciding to not be with each other in secluded places or having other people around if you have to be in such environments. My advice is to find what works for you and keep at it.

Deal with the attitude

When I was a little girl, I never really knew how to defend myself. Whenever I was faced with a situation where I had to speak for myself, I would cringe in fear and shed a lot of tears because I just could not handle such tension. As I grew older, life taught me that crying does not bring about the desired result or solution; I just have to face the situation as it comes. So, I knew it was time to toughen up, and I did. Maybe I went too far because when such situations arose, all I did was fight back the tears or fight through my tears, thereby getting defensive and angry. As a result, although I would be trying to defend myself, I was still unable to get my point across because it would then become an argument. This, I battled with for so long and developed an ungodly attitude from it. I ended up being full of resentment for people who don't agree with me or when things are not going my way, I would be ready with a defence for why it should be my way and not theirs.

The Formula: 1 + 1 = 1

I have learnt that love and such attitudes do not mix! This is because the devil is looking for an open door and when such attitudes are in one's life, they breed contempt, anger, strife, malice and the likes. In other words, you are simply opening a door to the enemy to enter what is a potential instrument in God's hands – your life. Don't allow that! Deal with the attitude before it deals with you. If you find yourself in a heated moment with your fiancé or fiancée, try to end the conversation. Take a walk; a long one until you have completely calmed down, and then come back to it. Use that time to also think of a better way to pass your message across. It's never about winning; it's always about making peace and allowing that peace to reign in your relationship. That's exactly what the enemy is trying to prevent, so you must war against any opposition. It is not normal. It is spiritual and you must deal with it as such.

Chapter 8

A FINAL WORD

As I come to the end of this book, my thoughts turn to the younger, upcoming or next generation. Whatever we choose to call them, the fact is that they are coming so close behind especially in this fast-paced digital world we have come to know. The best gift that we can give to them is the gift of lessons – everything you and I may have read or learnt will probably be more valuable to them. There's that school of thought that personal experience in the best teacher, but believe me when I say that you are never going to experience everything there is to learn in life before you grow old. Hence, we must create room for them to learn from life lessons that others have shared or handed down to us.

In this last chapter, I outline some of the lessons I have learnt that I would've loved my 16-year old self to know before reaching certain points of reckoning in life. Feel free to share these with any youngsters you may know or if you are raising any yourself:

1. God is the ultimate source of your life. Don't bother to 'branch' elsewhere. Just go directly to Him.

2. The more of God you know, the more of yourself you begin to know. Since there is no end to His mystery, what does that tell you about yourself?

3. There is something you were created for. Discover it and everything else will fall into place.

4. You can run but you can't hide from the plan of God for your life. If you don't seek it out, it will seek you out! Don't wait for that to happen. It can be explosive! Ask Jonah (Jonah 1-3).

5. It doesn't matter how much you think you have failed or messed up, God has a back-up plan because He can never be stranded. He has already made allowances for the times you might give up or get fed up. So, don't be afraid to make mistakes.

Scriptures to note

In addition to these nuggets, let me share five key Bible verses that I came to know and love as I grew older:

A Final Word

1. Ecclesiastes 12:1

Remember now your Creator in the days of your youth; before the difficult days come, and the years draw near when you say, 'I have no pleasure in them'.

2. 1 Timothy 4:12

Let no one despise your youth, but be an example to the believers in word, in conduct, in love, in spirit, in faith, in purity.

3. Proverbs 1:10

My son, if sinners entice you, do not consent.

4. Isaiah 55:6

Seek the LORD while He may be found, call upon Him while He is near.

5. 2 Timothy 2:22

Flee also youthful lusts: but follow righteousness, faith, charity, peace, with them that call on the Lord out of a pure heart.

I encourage you to read these scriptures on your own and think on them. You will get through life much more easily if you have these words of wisdom embedded on the tablet of your heart.

SINGLE AND WHOLE

Make them your life motto and let them guide the decisions you make. I see you attaining great heights as you live by these standards.

THE SINGLES CREED

A declaration

I am single and whole.

I live an enjoyable single life.

I am not sad, lonely or miserable.

I enjoy the season that I am in; it's the process for where I am going.

God is preparing me for whom He has prepared for me;

I will be an asset and not a deficit to him or her.

God is bringing me a man or woman who will take me higher not lower.

He or she will be an asset and not a deficit to me.

Therefore, I will not settle for anything less;

I will settle for God's best for me.

I am encouraged!

SINGLE AND WHOLE

I am strong!

I am not alone because God will never leave me nor forsake me.

God is taking me through the process and I will come out better and stronger, ready for the palace.

Amen.

NOTES

NOTES

www.ingramcontent.com/pod-product-compliance
Lightning Source LLC
Chambersburg PA
CBHW071324040426
42444CB00009B/2076